Anonymous

Great North Atlantic telegraph route

Anonymous

Great North Atlantic telegraph route

ISBN/EAN: 9783337147525

Printed in Europe, USA, Canada, Australia, Japan

Cover: Foto ©Andreas Hilbeck / pixelio.de

More available books at **www.hansebooks.com**

GREAT NORTH ATLANTIC

TELEGRAPH ROUTE.

COPYRIGHT.

LONDON:

PRINTED BY WILLIAM CLOWES AND SONS,

STAMFORD STREET AND CHARING CROSS.

1866.

THE following pages are a *résumé* of the experience and opinions of those Navigators and men of science who, from their researches in the regions about to be traversed by a Telegraphic Cable, or from the evidence they have received, are well qualified to judge as to the feasibility and practicability of the successful accomplishment of a North Atlantic Telegraphic Route.

London, January, 1866.

Julianeshaab.

THE PROPOSED STATION OF THE NORTH ATLANTIC TELEGRAPH
IN
Greenland.

TELEGRAPH ROUTE.

THE time has arrived when the civilized world demands, and the interest and wants of mankind require, that an attempt should be made to establish a telegraphic communication between Europe and America by a route which, although not without some physical difficulties, seems to be the only one which offers all the elements of permanence and success without enormous cost and hazardous risk.

The Atlantic Telegraph Company, with indomitable perseverance, have made three unsuccessful attempts to lay a telegraphic cable from the shores of Ireland to the coasts of Newfoundland, and have expended 1,900,000*l.* in a series of trials to make a communication (dependent upon a single line of telegraphic cable) between the two hemispheres. These noble efforts are deserving of every success and of every reward, yet the electric transmission between the old world and the new should not be dependent upon a single line of telegraphic cable.

It is proposed to form an Association to lay down a line of telegraphic wires from London, through Scot-

land, Shetland, and the Færöe Islands, to Iceland and
the western shores of Greenland, across Davis Straits
to the coast of Labrador or Belle Isle, and to communicate through Canada with the vast telegraphic system
of the United States and the continent of America.

This natural series of stations and electric circuits
in the North Atlantic can be combined in one grand
electric chain, by short and manageable sections of
land wires and submarine telegraphic cables, and the
distance between station and station is much within
the limits in which telegraphic cables are now successfully and profitably employed, the longest stretch of the
North Atlantic route being little more than 700 miles.

The distances between the stations are, proxi-
mately :—

		Miles.
Scotland to the Færöe Islands	. . .	250
Færöe to Iceland (Berufiord)	. . .	240
Iceland to Greenland	. . . . . .	743
Greenland to Labrador	. . . . .	507
Labrador to Canada (land line), or		
Greenland to Belle Isle (sea-line) . .		210

The sea route to America will thus be divided into
four portions, and the great advantages to be derived
by these divisions are very obvious. It will enable
duplicate cables to be laid throughout its whole
length ; one cable to be used for the outward, and
one for the return messages ; should mischance occur
to one cable the communication will not be suspended ;
and should both cables be in good working order, the

rapid transmission of messages would be much facili-
tated; the delays in the extreme cases of magnetic
storms reduced, and the permanence of electric communication assured.

Professor Wheatstone's opinion of December 1,
1865, is:—" Should the Northern Atlantic cable be
successfully laid, there can be no doubt of the great
advantage it would have in one important respect—
viz. that by means of its separate portions a more
speedy communication of intelligence would be effected than by the long sea-route, the impediments to
the rapid succession of signals having been proved to
be in proportion to the length of the conductor."

The experience of existing lines has defined the
velocity with which electricity travels through submerged metallic wires of different lengths under known
conditions, and also the general laws which influence
the retardation of the current in submarine cables.

Through the cables proposed to be laid down by
this route, electric transmission can be rapidly effected;
for example, through the Black Sea cable, a length
of 310 knots, 17 words per minute were sent from
Varna to Balaklava. (4,486. *Evidence before the Submarine Telegraph Committee.*)

With the knowledge now possessed, and by the
employment of suitable apparatus, there can be little
doubt that through the longest section of cable of the
North Atlantic route—*viz.* that between Iceland and
Greenland, a distance of 743 miles—electric trans-
missions equivalent to a speed of at least 15 words

per minute can be effected, whilst with the shorter sections of the cable a much higher speed, of from 20 to 30 words per minute, will be obtained.

The Atlantic Telegraph Company, through the Atlantic cable, which was successfully submerged in August, 1858, transmitted messages at the rate of $2\frac{1}{2}$ words per minute, and by comparing the maximum speed upon this continuous length of 2,500 miles with the rate attained upon submerged cables of shorter lengths, the capacity of every circuit proposed by the North Atlantic route may be ascertained.

" The capacity of every circuit that will be on the northern route is known by their equals in length already operating in deep seas; we have nothing to experiment upon, nothing to invent or discover." (4,138. *Submarine Telegraph Committee, March* 14, 1860, p. 238.)

The favourable electric working of the North Atlantic line is demonstrated by these facts, and its results commercially, as a remunerative undertaking, may be estimated by comparing the revenue to be derived from the ascertained working the Cable of the Atlantic Telegraph Company, through an unbroken line of 2,500 miles, from Valencia to Newfoundland :—

At $2\frac{1}{2}$ words per minute—

	£
For a working day of 16 hours, at	
5s. per word yields per day . .	600
Or per annum, for a year of 300 days	180,000

With the income to be earned by the North Atlantic Association, who, with the short lengths of cable and land lines will be enabled to transmit 15 words per minute:—

15 words per minute for a working
day of 16 hours, at 2s. 6d. per £
word, yields per day 1,800
Per annum, for a year of 300 days 540,000 ·

And it is probable that, owing to the differences of longitude, it may be found necessary to keep the line open day and night.

Although the line will be divided into sections, it will not be requisite to retransmit the through messages at each point of junction, but to place at each land station mechanical transmittors (repeating instruments), with relays of auxiliary battery power. England can thereby communicate with America without a break of line, in the same manner that London now communicates with Constantinople, Vienna, or St. Petersburg, and the telegraph clerks at the termination of each section of the cable will watch for and guard the safe transmission of the messages.

The comparatively small risk in the submersion of the cable, and the time required for that operation not exceeding a few days, and the small amount of labour and expense required for this portion of the work, are great advantages as compared with a long sea-line; also the probability of effecting insurances at moderate rates, for the safe submerging of the cables, as in the event of total loss, no cable will exceed 743 miles in length.

There is also the great facility for reparation and replacement of the cables should accident occur, the diminished cost of maintaining the short sections in working order, and the reduction of loss to the Association in the event of temporary failure in the laying down of the cables.

The Northern routes of the telegraphic cables are of much benefit and electric advantage. Telegraph lines work much better in cold climates than in warm latitudes; the telegraphic experience of the United States, extending over varied zones of temperature, has shown that in the southern portion of the United States, during the summer months, when the telegraph wires are heated by the action of the sun, the conductibility of the wires is lessened, and it is often necessary to diminish the electric currents. In the northern part of the United States, where the cold is sometimes greater than that of Greenland, the lines are worked with less battery power, and without interruption in cold weather, and it is found that during periods of severe cold the telegraphic transmission is most successful.

The map appended to this pamphlet delineates the proposed course of the lines, and the section shows the approximate depth of the ocean throughout the bed of the sea.

The maximum depth of the sea between *Scotland* and *Færöe* is 254 fathoms, and Sir Leopold M‘Clintock, who was appointed by the Government to make a survey of the line, states:—" I could not fail to observe that a submarine cable in connection with the main line and a land wire across could be maintained with perfect ease."

Between *Færöe* and *Iceland* the maximum depth

was 682 fathoms. Capt. Allen Young, who commanded the ' Fox,' upon the expedition sent out under the auspices of Lord Palmerston, says :—" There will be no difficulties from the sea, ice, or otherwise, and the only obstacles will be from fogs and thick weather, but which may be overcome by selecting proper seasons and taking precautions in landing or embarking the electric cable."

Between *Iceland* and *Greenland*, the maximum depth is 1,550 fathoms. Capt. Sir Leopold M'Clintock communicates an extract from a letter from the well-known Dr. Rink, resident Inspector-Governor of South Greenland (for the Danish Government) :—

" I have thought much over the proposed route for the North Atlantic Telegraph. At first I doubted the possibility of accomplishing it, but now I am of a contrary opinion. You can lay down the cable from Iceland, round Cape Farewell, into some fiord upon the south-west coast, where ice cannot ground upon it or touch it except for a few fathoms out from the shore, and this part may be easily protected."

Sir Leopold M'Clintock says, " It is evident that were a cable brought in from the deep water existing outside and between these Islands, and carried sufficiently far up a deep fiord, its security from icebergs would be ensured, and that to protect the mere shore end from ordinary flat ice would be a matter of no difficulty."

Capt. Allen Young says, " I am of decided opinion that a depth of not less than 150 to 160 fathoms can

be carried from the middle of the fiord abreast the
settlement (Julianshaab Fiord) out to sea with a general
muddy bottom. The depth of water will effectually
preclude injury to the cable from the icebergs ever
seen upon the coast. Although many bergs lay along
the coast, we saw none aground in this valley of the
fiord, nor, according to information obtained from
the residents, have they been seen grounded in the
channel. This report and my previous letters will
show that my decided opinion (so far as we have been
upon that route) is favourable to the practicability of
the undertaking, and that Julianshaab will, under all
circumstances, be well adapted for the reception of the
cable. With regard to the operation of laying the
cable, I consider that no apprehension may be felt on
that point ; for from the sudden disappearance which
we witnessed of the ice upon the coast, and from the
ice usually dispersing from the south-east of Greenland
in the autumnal months, opportunities will always
occur, when a ship having a cable on board, and
lying in readiness in Julianshaab, may depend upon
having a period of clear and open sea. The cable once
laid, no drift ice can in any way injure it if the proper
precautions are taken for securing the shore end."

*Extract of Paper read by J. W. TAYLOR, Esq., F.R.G.S.,
before the Royal Geographical Society.*

"From the results of seven years' observation in
Greenland, I am of opinion that neither the ice nor

the configuration of the coast will offer any impediment to the successful laying and landing of the telegraph cable in Greenland."

'The Times,' Dec. 5, 1860.

"The existence of ice-drift along the south coast is in reality no difficulty; it only prevails at the commencement of the season, except in an exceptional year such as that recently experienced (1860). Even when thickest, its movements with various winds are so perfectly understood, that under the command of experienced captains many frail ships, unadapted for ice navigation, visit and return from all parts of the coast usually in safety. With regard to the American terminus of the line, now that the Greenland difficulty has been removed, when once the line has been carried there in 50 meridian western longitude, the landing on the opposite shore can be selected on any point within some hundreds of miles, without increasing materially the length of the circuit."

FROM GREENLAND TO LABRADOR.

Sir Leopold M'Clintock says:—"The line of soundings to Hamilton Inlet shows that the greatest depth, which is mid-channel, is 2,032 fathoms, and that the decrease is very gradual until within 80 miles of Labrador, where there is a change from about 900 fathoms to 150 fathoms in 7 or 8 miles. The ocean bed consisted of ooze, but with fewer microscopic organisms than previously met with, whilst the average temperature of the sea at 100 fathoms below the surface was 40 degrees."

Capt. Norman, a Newfoundland merchant, who has traded at Hamilton Inlet, on the coast of Labrador, for twenty-four years, states that icebergs rarely enter the mouth of Hamilton Inlet, and never pass within the Hern Islands (at the entrance of the inlet) for these reasons :—

1. That the current which has borne them from the north is here deflected off shore by the Esquimaux Islands and carries them past the mouth of the inlet ; and 2nd, that the flow of water caused by the discharge of several large rivers into the inlet still further aids in carrying the drift-ice and the icebergs to sea-ward.

HAMILTON INLET TO MINGAN.

If it be desirable, the telegraph cable can be carried to Belle Isle instead of Hamilton Inlet. A company was formed in Montreal in the year 1860, in conjunction with the British and Canadian Telegraph Company, to lay down an independent cable to join the submarine line, and the soundings and observations taken by the Canadian Company satisfactorily prove the practicability of the line and the pecuniary advantages to be obtained from this portion of the line of telegraph.

This short summary of the evidence of disinterested and competent witnesses, proves, that no physical difficulty exists which may not be surmounted for the completion of a telegraphic cable throughout the proposed route. Appended is the impartial testimony of commanders of the British navy and officers of the Danish and mercantile marine, who have been employed for several years in the Greenland and Iceland seas, all well acquainted with the ice and the so-called dangers of the floating icebergs of these regions. The officers of the Danish marine annually visit the shores of Greenland, where a large trade is carried on, (the exportation of criolite alone amounting to 20,000 tons per annum,) and they are without exception in favour of the practicability, and are confident of the successful and permanent laying, of a telegraph cable from Greenland, Iceland, Færöe, and Labrador.

A few words may be necessary as to the presumed danger of the ice in these northern latitudes. It is well known that no ice of any kind is found in the seas between Scotland and Iceland. The testimony of the Danish and English navigators proves that no *Arctic* ice of any description is ever found on the southern shores of Iceland; that being the only shore of that island where the telegraphic cable would be landed.

The sea along the southern shore of Iceland is very seldom frozen; it happened four times only in the last century, namely, in 1717, 1742, 1784, 1792.

In Henderson's 'Iceland' (second edition, p. 9, page 273) it is stated, "At first I shuddered at the idea of spending a winter in Iceland, but what was my surprise when I found the temperature of the atmosphere not only greater than that of the preceding winter in Denmark, but equal to that of the mildest winter I have lived either in Sweden or Denmark."

The ice formed on the south shore of Iceland and of Newfoundland never exceeds one foot in thickness, and the freezing of the waters occurs much oftener in Newfoundland than in Iceland, yet the Atlantic Telegraph Company have not considered this any formidable obstacle, nor can ice of the before-named thickness do injury to a telegraphic cable, if the usual precautions are adopted at the landing places of the cable; it may be stated that the dangers from ice and icebergs are not greater than those to which the telegraphic cables are annually submitted in the Great and Little Belts and the Baltic Sea, yet in these waters submarine cables have been maintained, and have been successfully worked for many years.

The following geographical and hydrographical description of the seas and islands traversed by the proposed route, are extracted from the proceedings of the Royal Geographical Society, in January and February, 1861 :—

Lord ASHBURTON, President, said, " The papers which are about to be read relate altogether to the physical and geographical facts upon which the pro-position has been based for the extension of the Electric Telegraph line between this country and America, by the route of the Færöe Islands, Iceland, Greenland, and Labrador. The researches which we are met to record to-day were not for the purpose of acquiring geographical knowledge simply, but in order to carry out the great and beneficent scheme of connecting the two great continents of Europe and America by means of telegraphic communication."

1. *Surveys of H.M.S. Bulldog.* By Capt. Sir F. Leopold M'Clintock, R.N., F.R.G.S.

[Extracts.]

" Although my visit to the *Færöe Islands* was not for the purpose of making any examination of their shores, yet I could not fail to observe that a sub-marine cable, in connection with the main island, and a land-wire across it, could be maintained with perfect ease.

" On landing at Thorshaven, the chief town of the islands, I observed that the little bays near it afforded ample shelter and security for any cable landed within them.

" The east and west coasts of Iceland are very seldom visited by drift-ice, not oftener than seven or eight times in each century, whilst it is only upon two or three of these occasions that the drift of Arctic ice is sufficiently extensive to reach the south coast.

True icebergs are *never* seen; the masses sometimes mistaken for them are small enough to float in comparatively shallow water, so that a cable would remain undisturbed at the bottom, its shore-end being carried into a fiord. Faxe Bay, on the south-west coast, enjoys a remarkable exemption from drift-ice; the last mention of its appearance within it is as long as 1683: neither does it freeze over—merchant vessels trade there throughout the winter. A cable could therefore be landed in this bay with perfect ease and security, and probably to the westward of Reikiavik.

" Although Iceland is considerably larger than Ireland, and is of volcanic origin throughout, yet for long ages the disturbance occasioned by its subterranean fires has been limited almost exclusively to its south-western quarter. Fortunately the telegraph route is not required to pass, by sea or land, through any part of this disturbed or suspected area.

" The nature of the bottom was chiefly ooze, that is, fine mud partly consisting of minute organic remains; but near to Iceland volcanic mud and sand were more frequently brought up. The temperature of the sea at 100 fathoms below the surface gradually diminished from 46 degrees near Iceland, to 39 degrees off the Greenland coast.

" The *Greenland* shore, within 45 miles of it, the depth was ascertained to be 1,175 fathoms. The line of soundings to Hamilton Inlet shows that the greatest depth—which is in mid-channel—is 2,032 fathoms; and the decrease is very gradual until within about

80 miles of Labrador, where there is a change from about 900 fathoms to 150 fathoms in 7 or 8 miles.

" The ocean-bed consisted of oaze, but with fewer microscopic organisms than previously met with, whilst the average temperature of the sea at 100 fathoms below the surface was 40 degrees.

" The greater part of the local information which I obtained here was kindly furnished by Capt. Norman, a Newfoundland merchant, who has traded here each successive summer for twenty-four years; during the summer he resides at Indian Harbour, at the north entrance of the inlet, where there is a secure anchorage for vessels of moderate size. Capt. Norman states that icebergs very rarely enter the mouth of the Hamilton Inlet, and never pass within the Hern Islets; and for these reasons: 1st, that the current which has borne them from the north is here deflected off shore by the Esquimaux Islands, and carries them past the mouth of the inlet; and 2ndly, that the flow of water caused by the discharge of several large rivers into the inlet still further aids in carrying the drift-ice and icebergs out to seaward.

" At the *Hudson Bay* trading-post upon North-West River, at the head of the inlet, I met Mr. Smith, the gentleman in charge, who seemed to think there would be no difficulty in carrying a wire from here overland to Mingan, on the gulf of St. Lawrence.

" Leaving Labrador on the 17th September, I returned to Greenland for the purpose of completing such

c 2

soundings as the drift-ice had previously compelled me to leave undone.

"The season was very remarkable for the great quantity of drift-ice which encumbered the shore, and had hitherto prevented vessels from approaching *Julianshaab*, in fact, so much ice had not been known for nearly thirty years. This coast, I may remark, is usually quite free from ice by September. Following up my inquiries, I learned that the climate is not nearly so severe as is generally supposed, the fiords are only partially frozen over in winter; a few cows, goats, and poultry are reared; and although the summers are cold, turnips, spinach lettuce, and radishes grow in the open air.

"I was informed that the large fiord of *Tessermiut*, which lies midway between *Julianshaab* and *Cape Farewell*, was the most likely place to afford security for a cable; that icebergs never came into it, and that there would be found ample depth of water from it out to sea; also that there is safe anchorage in a spacious bay near its mouth as well as high up in the fiord.

"It is well known that a current from the North Atlantic Ocean bears along with it all this ice round *Cape Farewell*, and up the west coast of *Greenland* for several hundred miles. It carries the drift-ice for the most part along the outer islands, and it is only when there is a strong wind blowing in from the sea that the ice comes in between the islands and enters the fiords; it is almost exclusively low or flat ice which thus drifts in, the larger masses and icebergs which draw more water, nearly always keep in the main stream along the outer islands.

"It is evident that were a cable brought in from the deep water existing outside and between these islands, and carried sufficiently far up a deep fiord, its security from icebergs would be ensured ; and that to protect the mere shore-end from the ordinary flat-ice would be a matter of no great difficulty.

"Since my return to England I have received a letter from the Resident Inspector of South Greenland, the well-known *Dr. Rink,* whose writings on *Greenland* have added so largely to our knowledge of the physical condition of that great Arctic Continent. The opinion of such a man deserves serious attention, since it is scarcely possible to quote a higher authority upon the point in question. I therefore do so almost in his own words.

"'I have thought much,' he writes, 'over the proposed route for the North Atlantic Telegraph ; at first I doubted the possibility of accomplishing it, but now I am of a contrary opinion. You can lay down the cable from Iceland round Cape Farewell into some fiord upon the south-west coast, where ice cannot ground upon it, or touch it except for a few fathoms out from the shore, and this last part may be easily protected. But to carry the wire across the interior of Greenland, as I have heard of, would be impracticable.' This letter was written in Greenland, before either the 'Bulldog' or 'Fox' had arrived there, and experience

has since shown the necessity for acting in accordance
with the suggestion of Rink.

"Once laid in deep water, the North Atlantic
Cable will probably be more secure and more durable
than any other, as it will lie at the bottom of a sea
where the temperature is unusually low, and where
animal life is proportionately rare.

"Judging, then, from my own experience, and from
the facts which the voyage of the 'Bulldog' has brought
to light—many of which are supported by the most
reliable local authorities—I am of opinion that with
regard to the practicability of laying a North Atlantic
cable there are no grounds for serious misgivings; on
the contrary, nearly all the information which has so
far been ascertained is of a kind favourable to the accomplishment of the undertaking."

2. *Extracts from Synopsis of the Surveys of the ' Fox,'
under the command of* Capt. ALLEN YOUNG, F.R.G.S.
Presented by Sir CHARLES J. BRIGHT, F.R.S.

FÆRÖE ISLANDS.

This group of isles lies some 200 miles north of
Scotland, and is under the authority of the Danish
Crown.

" When 46 miles E.S.E. from Naalsöe we obtained
soundings in 102 fathoms, sand and shells.

" *Thorshaven* (the capital) and bay is protected by
Naalsöe, and is land-locked, excepting on two points

to the south-east, and on one point to the north-east. The bay has good anchorage, varying in depth from 25 to 8 fathoms, bottom of sand, gravel, and shells, with a few patches of hard ground. Either of the inner harbours would do very well to land the telegraph wires; but half-a-mile southward of Thorshaven is a small cove called Sandygerde, where the cable could be landed in safety and clear of ships' anchors."

ICELAND.

Beru Fiord.—" *No icebergs have ever been seen on the coast.* The drift-ice appears with northerly, and departs with southerly winds, and less of it comes into Beru Fiord than any other fiord on the east coast of Iceland. The fiord itself never freezes, but thin ice has been known to cover the harbour off the factory for a day or two during the winter.

"There will be no difficulties from the sea, ice, or otherwise, and the only obstacles will be from fogs and thick weather, but which may be overcome by selecting proper seasons, and taking precautions in landing or embarking the telegraph cable.

Hval Fiord.—" I proceeded up that fiord, sounding it as far as 'Maria Havn,' a small harbour and salmon river on the south shore, seven miles from the entrance of the fiord. The least depth of water in the channel of the fiord is 14 fathoms, with deeper water both outside and in the general depth, being 18 to 20 fathoms, soft mud. The cable could be taken into Maria Havn

through soft mud, on a sandy beach, in a landlocked
position. Hval Fiord is protected from a heavy sea
breaking into it by the shoals of ' Vestrhram,' and
' Sydiahraun ' in Faxe Bay, and on which there is less
water than in the shoalest part of the channel in the
fiord. The bays in the fiord are sometimes covered
with thin ice, but the fiord itself never freezes; and
with reference to the drift-ice on this part of the coast,
I cannot do better than quote the words of Sir Leopold
M'Clintock, ' Faxe Bay never freezes over, and I can
find no record of drift-ice within since 1683. Merchant
vessels come and go throughout the winter.' "

GREENLAND.

Julianshaab Fiord.—"I am of a decided opinion
that *a depth of not less than* 150 to 160 *fathoms* can be
carried from the middle of the fiord abreast the settlement, out to sea, with a general muddy bottom.

" *The depth of water will effectually preclude injury
to the cable from the largest icebergs ever seen upon the
coast.* Although many bergs lay along the coast, we
saw none aground in this valley of the fiord, nor, according to information obtained from the residents,
have they been seen grounded in that channel. This
report, and my previous letters, will show that my
decided opinion (so far as we have been upon that
route) is favourable to the practicability of the undertaking, and that *Julianshaab* will, under all circumstances, be well adapted for the reception of the cable.

With regard to the operation of laying the cable, I consider that no apprehension may be felt on that point, for, from the sudden disappearance which we witnessed of the ice from the coast, and from the ice *usually* dispersing from the south-east shores of Greenland in the autumnal months, opportunities will always occur when a ship, having the cable on board, and lying in readiness in Julianshaab, may depend upon having a period of clear and open sea. *The cable once laid, no drift-ice can in any way injure it if the proper precautions are taken in securing the shore end.*

Ice of the Greenland Seas.—"Since my arrival I have seen the admirable remarks of Mr. J. W. Taylor upon the southern coast of Greenland, the results of his experience during seven years' residence there. His opinions must be most satisfactory to you, and I am sure that all who are interested in the work must be grateful to him for having so freely given them.

"With reference to Faxe Bay station, the west coast of Iceland is generally free from fogs, and the gulf stream which sets round Cape Reikianess, and appears to keep up a continuous flow round Cape Faxe Bay to the northward, passing out by Snœfellssness, also appears to considerably affect the climatic condition of the west coast. Navigation is open all the year round, and the operation of bringing the cable here can be timed to the opportunities for departing from Greenland."

Extract of Paper read by Dr. JOHN RAE.

"The population of Iceland amounts at present to some 60,000; at one time it is said to have been as high as 100,000, but the ravages of epidemic diseases and other causes reduced the numbers to less than those at present on the island.

"The masses of the people are able and active, harmless and honest. Wherever we went we were received with much kindness and hospitality, and even at the poorest cottages milk, coffee, and brandy were handed to us. All classes seem more or less educated, and the Lutheran religion prevails.

"The price of labour varies from 1*s*. 2*d*. to 2*s*. 8*d*. per day, according to the season. During the hay-making, in the months of July, August, and September, it is highest.

"The result of this expedition, as far as regards the land portion of it over the Færöe Isles and Iceland, was extremely favourable to the practicability of laying down or erecting a telegraphic wire. The question in Iceland will be, whether the telegraph should be carried across the whole island from Beru Fiord to Faxe Bay, or only from Portland Bay to the latter place. The latter will reduce the distance on land from about 250 to 90 miles."

Adjourned Discussion on the North Atlantic Telegraph Papers.

"Sir EDWARD BELCHER thought, in the first instance, as has been proved, that they should find a great connecting bank between Scotland and the Færöes, and between Iceland and Greenland. As to the difficulties which were raised with reference to the Labrador shore, he was very glad to find that the reefs, which it was said would entirely prevent any cable being laid across there, have vanished with the ice; they have gone southerly somewhere or other and have not yet been found; at least those reefs that are there are rather helps than otherwise, by preventing the ice coming down upon the entrance.

"Mr. PLINY MILES—Iceland is not so cold as might be imagined, from its name and locality. With regard to the thickness of ice at Reikiavik, he had a distinct recollection that the lake spoken of is seldom known to be frozen to the depth of 18 inches. He had been told that sometimes it was not frozen more than 2 inches during the whole course of the winter, showing most conclusively the mildness of the climate.

"Captain SHERARD OSBORN, R.N. — The distinguished travellers and navigators, who read their papers at the last meeting, have given us sufficient authority to say that there were obstacles on the route undoubtedly, but that all those obstacles are surmountable. Touching the soundings, he would call the attention of the meeting to the agreeable fact that the entire line of soundings show that there is no depth greater than 1,000 fathoms between Scotland and longitude 30° W. on the proposed route, or exactly half-way across the Atlantic Ocean. There are then two valleys of deep water, of small width, on either side of Greenland.

The soundings diminish very abruptly as Greenland is approached, and shallow water will be found probably round Cape Farewell. With regard to the Labrador coast, the principal difficulty was in carrying the cable within the 150 fathoms of water, so that it might not be exposed to the action of the icebergs. He was sure that arctic men all agree that 150 fathoms would be about the maximum draught of any iceberg, so that the chief object to be secured in placing the cable is to push the 150 fathom mark as near into the coast as possible. No man would dispute that bergs of ice sounding the bottom would rip it up, just as a plough would a ploughed field, and that if that bank was thus ripped up by the floes of ice there would be hardly any animal or vegetable life upon it; it would be a kind of subterranean desert. Sir Leopold M'Clintock was continually dredging there, and in a note just received, that distinguished navigator said, ' The bank of Hamilton Inlet has from 100 to 200 fathoms upon it. I am of opinion that icebergs which ever drift down there cannot possibly reach the bottom. They ground near the islands at the entrance, and are not bergs of the largest size. Shells and other small things were brought up by the sounding machines in 40 or 50 fathoms *as in other parts of the sea* where icebergs cannot possibly interfere with them.' Near Frederickshaab Captain Sir L. M'Clintock says they dredged up, in 26 fathoms, delicate corals and creatures which could not live at the bottom of the sea if much disturbed by icebergs; and adds, ' *so much for the destructive propensities of icebergs.*' There were remarks at the last meeting about difficulties with regard to the intense cold and the aurora borealis affecting the telegraph. It might be interesting for the Society to know that a few seasons ago Captain Kellett and Captain M'Clintock were beset in the ice in 74½° N., and they communicated WITH EACH OTHER BY TELE-GRAPH FROM SHIP TO SHIP. Now 74½° N. latitude was a long way in the Arctic zone, and the cable, the practicability of which they were at present discussing, would lie a long way without it. That telegraph was at work throughout the whole winter, and was not in any way affected by that terrible bugbear, the aurora borealis, nor by the intense cold experienced so far north.

" SIR RODERICK MURCHISON.—They were not there to discuss engineering merits of the project, but they were capable of estimating, in a very decisive manner, the facts that Sir Leopold M'Clintock and Capt. Sherard Osborn, who are men of great experience as Arctic voyagers, have pronounced in favour of this scheme. Not having any pecuniary interest in it, or in any rival speculation, he might say to the gentlemen of the North Atlantic Company, they had put their case so well before the public that no gentleman associated with other lines. could say that they had not treated the subject in a most ingenuous and fair manner.

" DR. RAE did not profess to be a surveyor, but having travelled a good deal both in the United States and Canada, he had seen telegraphs carried over more difficult and rougher country than they encountered in crossing Iceland. But should objections be offered to carrying the telegraph completely across the island, he was of opinion, from information obtained, that Portland, in the south of Iceland, although no safe harbour for ships, would form a good landing-place for a cable. From Portland to Reikiavik the distance is not over 20 miles, and the road offers no obstacles."

Public attention has been for some time directed to the North Atlantic route as the most desirable course for European and American telegraph connection, but the existence of concessions granted by the Danish Government, the possessors of which did not, from various causes, exercise the power they possessed, prevented the formation of a powerful Association with the necessary capital to undertake and complete the telegraphic line, and the necessary stations upon the land and through the sea. A short history of these attempts to secure concessions for the route is subjoined :—

In 1852, Mr. Wyld, M.P., applied to the Danish Government for permission to use the Danish territories for establishing a telegraphic line between England and America, and M. Reventlow, in a letter dated August, 1852, stated that the Danish Government " will have no objection to your laying your wires through those of the Danish territories which are in your way."

In 1854, Col. Shaffner, an American citizen, obtained a concession to "establish a telegraphic line from North America by the way of Greenland, Iceland, the Færöe Islands, and thence *via* Norway and Sweden, to *Copenhagen*, which shall be the only point of termination of such telegraphic establishment." This concession was dormant until the year 1859, when Mr. Campbell, M.P., Chairman of the Great Eastern Steamship, James Wyld, M.P., and Thomas Page, C.E., applied to the Danish Government for permission to land telegraphic cables on the Danish territories, and to connect the cable with the shores of Great Britain ; and as Col. Shaffner had made no progress in carrying out the concession granted to him, the application of these English gentlemen was favourably received, and they had good reasons for believing that the government of Denmark would grant to them, if not an exclusive right, at least a permissive right to land telegraph Cables on the shores of Færöe, Iceland, and Greenland. But the publicity given to this application attracted the attention of Col. Shaffner, who appeared in Copenhagen in 1859, and obtained an extension of time for the fulfilment of the terms of his concession, and upon the deposit of 100,000 dollars, under this new arrangement, permission was granted to land the line upon the coasts of Scotland, but was fettered by the condition " that the line from the Færöe Islands to Scotland be only used for correspondence between North America on the one side, and Great Britain and Ireland on the other side, consequently not for the correspondence between North America and the continent of Europe, this correspondence being exclusively reserved to the line conducted to Denmark, whichever the two said ways this line may take."

Differences having arisen amongst the parties with whom Col. Shaffner was associated, the caution money was refunded by the Danish Government, and the concession cancelled.

The intervention of Col. Shaffner prevented Mr. Wyld, who was the original projector of this line, and those who acted with him from heretofore attempting to complete and carry out this route; but in the autumn of last year (1865), the Danish Government granted to Mr. Wyld, and some gentlemen whom he associated with him, a concession, which, cancelling all existing concessions, gives to Mr. Wyld and his associates the exclusive right, for a term of years, to lay down telegraphic cables throughout the Danish dominions in Europe and in America, and at the end of that time leaves the existing proprietors of the line in possession of their line, and all the property and buildings they may possess. The Concession also abnegates the stringent stipulations of Col. Shaffner's concessions, which made Denmark the telegraphic centre of the communications between Europe and America, and permits the cables to be laid from any part of the coasts of Great Britain and Ireland to and from the Danish territories.

Telegraphic communication with America is a

social and commercial necessity, and the liberal concession granted by the Danish Government has removed the obstacles which before existed. The explorations and surveys made by order of Her Majesty's Government, by Sir Leopold McClintock in the 'Bulldog,' and the surveys and observations of Capt. Allen Young, Mr. Davis, and others in the steamship 'Fox,' are highly satisfactory.

The annexed reports of the officers of the Danish navy, and of the commanders of ships employed in the Danish Greenland trade, leave no doubt as to the practicability of the route.

The favourable opinions of the leading scientific men of England, whose testimony is appended, are guarantees to the public for the integrity of the undertaking, and the evidence given before the Commission appointed by the Board of Trade to investigate the subject of Submarine Telegraphy, is conclusive as to the possibility of laying a cable through the land and seas of the North Atlantic route.

APPENDIX.

NORTH ATLANTIC ROUTE.

Scientific Testimony, received December, 1865.

SIR RODERICK IMPEY MURCHISON, Bart., F.R.S., *President of the Royal Geographical Society, &c. &c. &c.*

"Judging from the opinions of Sir Leopold M'Clintock, Dr. Wallick, Capt. Allen Young, and Dr. Rae, who assisted in the preliminary survey of the North Atlantic route, and from the discussions which have taken place in the Royal Geographical Society, I am led to believe that this line of telegraphic communication can be satisfactorily established.

(Signed)   "RODERICK J. MURCHISON."

MAJOR-GENERAL SABINE, *President of the Royal Society, &c. &c. &c.*

"I do not apprehend that any serious inconvenience would be occasioned by magnetic storms to the working of the North Atlantic Cable, beyond that which is sometimes experienced from the same cause in England.

(Signed)   "EDWARD SABINE."

PROFESSOR WHEATSTONE, F.R.S., D.C.L., &c. &c. &c.

"Should the Northern Atlantic Cable be successfully laid, there can be no doubt of the great advantage it would have in one important respect, *viz.* that by means of its separate portions a more speedy communication of intelligence would be effected than by the long sea route, the impediments to the rapid succession of signals having been proved to be in proportion to the length of the conductor.

(Signed)   "C. WHEATSTONE."

CAPT. M. F. MAURY, *the eminent Deep Sea Geographer.*

"Captain M. F. Maury has no hesitation in stating that this route does not present any insurmountable difficulties in laying a cable to America.

(Signed)   "By CAPTAIN MAURY's request,
"J. W. TREMLETT."

D 2

CAPT. ALLEN YOUNG, R.N., *Commander of North Atlantic Telegraph Expedition of* 1860.

"I have no reason to depart from the favourable opinion I expressed in the report, which I made when I returned from the survey of North Atlantic Telegraph route in 1860.

(Signed) "ALLEN YOUNG,

"*Late Commander of North Atlantic Telegraph Expedition in the 'Fox,' and in conjunction with H.M.S. 'Bulldog.'*"

CAPT. DAVIS, R.N., *Staff Commander and Surveyor to the North Atlantic Expedition of* 1860.

"As Surveyor of the North Atlantic Expedition, under Captain Allen Young, it is my opinion, that with proper care it is perfectly feasible and safe to lay a Telegraphic Cable by the Northern Route as far as Greenland, to which coast my examination extended, and that, owing to the great depth of water in the fiords, there is no danger whatever to be apprehended from icebergs.

(Signed) "J. E. DAVIS,

"*Staff-Commander, R.N., and Surveyor to the North Atlantic Expedition in the 'Fox,' in conjunction with H.M.S. 'Bulldog,' 1860.*"

DR. WALLICK, *Naturalist to the Expedition on board H.M.S. 'Bulldog.*

"Having examined the soundings taken during the survey of the North Atlantic Telegraph Route by H.M.S. 'Bulldog' in 1860, I beg to state it as my opinion, that although animal life undoubtedly exists down to the greatest depths recorded, it presents no characters which are likely to prove injurious to a submerged cable.

(Signed) G. C. WALLICK, M.D.,

"*Late Naturalist to the Expedition on board H.M.S. 'Bulldog.'*"

DEAR SIR,—In compliance with a request in your letter of 18th, I have the pleasure to state, that—

Founded upon my general knowledge of Greenland, and upon my own personal experiences during a year's residence in that country, where, in 1863, I was ordered on a surveying expedition (commanded by Captain Falbe), along the coasts of Greenland, I am positively convinced of the possibility and the practicability of undertaking a telegraphic line across the Færöe Islands, Iceland, and Greenland.

> I remain, dear Sir,
> Your most obedient Servant,
> E. BLUHME, R.D.N.

To JAMES WYLD, M.P., K. of several Orders.

MR. WYLD,—It is with the greatest pleasure that I—as you ask my opinion about the possibility of laying down a transatlantic cable *viâ* the west coast of Greenland—can assure you that, after the experience I have gathered on the coasts of this land in the years 1862-65, I regard such an enterprise as fully practicable, when the right season is chosen and assistance of people well known in the Arctic zone is secured. What the west coast of Iceland concern, I have visited it three times, and I do not believe that you will meet with any difficulties here. As to the detail, I refer to the following letter.

> Remaining, Sir,
> Your obedient Servant,
> CARLE NORMANN, R.D.N.

Copenhagen, November 18th, 1865.

S.S.

Hr. WYLD,—Paa deres Foresporgsmaal til mig, der som Skibsforer i en længere Aarrakke har beseilet den grönlandske Kyst, angaaende min mening om muligheden af at udlægge en Telegraphtraad fra denne, er det mig kjært at kunne meddele Dem, at jeg anseer dette Foretagende for fuldkommen prakticabelt, og ikke troer at Isen, naar det rette Oieblik vælges, kan frembyde nogen Hindring, der ikke kan overvindes. Fra hvilket Punkt man imidlertid bör gaae ud tör jeg ikke indlade mig paa at besvare.

> med Höiagtelse,
> erbödigst,
> P. J. PETERSEN,
> *Skibsförer.*

Kbhvn, 17er November, 1865.

TRANSLATION.

Hr. WYLD,—With regard to your inquiry of me as a Captain who has been engaged for a number of years in the Greenland trade, as to my opinion with regard to laying a Telegraph Cable from the Greenland coast, I am pleased to be able to report that I consider the same (to be) perfectly practicable, and I do not doubt but that if the right moment is only used the ice cannot present any obstacle that cannot be overcome; but from which point the cable should be started I am not prepared to state.

———

Mr. WYLD,—As you have requested me to express my opinion of the possibility of placing a submarine cable between Iceland and Greenland, and Greenland and Labrador, I take the liberty to send you these lines.

I have, in the years 1862-65, three times visited the south coast of Greenland in the 'Fox' steamer, the same vessel so famously known from the expedition of Sir Leopold M'Clintock, to find the remains of Sir John Franklin and his companions, and in the above-mentioned years I have spent more than four months in different creeks of this country, and in or near the ice which you nearly always find surrounding this coast. I tell you this, in order to let you know from where I have got my knowledge to this generally unknown country.

I do consider the placement of a cable on the coast of Greenland not only as a possibility, but even as a not very difficult undertaking, when the due moment and the right means are selected. The only difficulty in the undertaking must be sought in the ice, but this you may nearly quite avoid if the right season is selected.

It is notorious that every spring large quantities of field ice, formed by the coasts of Spitzbergen, are carried by the Arctic current along the east coast of Greenland. In the month of April they pass the Cape Farewell, and in May, June, and July they sometimes trouble the navigation of South Greenland, but from the commencement of August, they considerably decrease, and it is very unusual that the navigation, after the middle of this month, is at all made difficult by the ice. The time of my visits on the coasts of Greenland were, on all my voyages, in the most unfavourable season, and the one of them even in an uncommonly unfortunate moment, but the ice would never have prevented the putting down of a cable on the *western* side of the south coast; nay, in July, 1862, and in August, 1865, such an undertaking would not even have met with more difficulties than the laying down of a cable between England and France. In October, 1865, I passed the "icebelt," hardly without seeing ice, although we for a long time had had easterly storms that might have brought down the ice from the east coast. I hope you, from this, will feel sure that the field ice will not be able to harm your enterprise.

Another thing is if the "icebergs" will be an obstacle to the undertaking. I certainly don't think so when one of the exceedingly deep fiords of South Greenland, as Tessermint Fgalliko or Arsuk, is selected as starting-point. In the first of these there is nowhere to be found less than 100 fathoms of water; in the second the depth is about the same; and in the third I have sounded myself, and to the south of the Arsuk island I had no bottom in 120 fathoms, a few cables' length from the shore. In such depths there is no danger for the icebergs taking ground, and the fear is still lessened when we remember that the depth of the sea outside the fiords is still greater, and that icebergs are very seldom seen in these, as they generally remain in the current.

If I am asked, How is the coast of Greenland, and how is the bottom near the coast? I must answer, That the coast is exceedingly well for the bringing ashore, and the placing of a telegraph cable, and that I likewise have found the bottom of the sea at some places as level as that of the Danish Sound.

The fact that a number of vessels (twenty-eight in 1865) yearly arrives at Iviglict, Arsuk Fyord, is a better proof than anything else that there can be no considerable difficulty in the navigation of the coast, for the greatest number of these vessels have even only been single-bottomed sailing-ships. These vessels that come to the above-mentioned harbour to fetch Kryolith go in ballast from Europe and America, and would be very glad to take materials, &c., to the telegraph station for a moderate freight.

From what I have said you see that I, without being sanguine, consider the putting down of a cable from the coast of Greenland as quite practicable, but still I think quite necessary.

1. That a place on the *South-west* coast of Greenland is selected as starting point, the east coast only exceptionally being approachable, and that the vessel is amply supplied with cable, as the ice possibly may prevent her going the shortest way.

2. That the starting of the cable must be commenced from the coast of Greenland, a look-out with the ice being able from here so as to choose the favourable moments that current and wind may offer, and from here having the greatest probability of having fair wind during the passage.

3. That a strong, double-bottomed steamer is sent with the cable (I dare say it will be profitable to lay down at once the two lines—Iceland, Greenland, Labrador—from two different ships) together with another strong, well-constructed steamer, as aviso.

4. The expedition must leave England as early as possible, and be guided by men who have been formerly in Arctic seas, and who know the localities.

I have now expressed to you, Sir, my opinion of your plan to the laying down of a telegraph cable *viâ* Greenland ; and I feel proud to have been able to contribute my share to a scheme of so great interest to the whole civilized world. I heartily wish you success to so great an undertaking, and I feel convinced that you will and must succeed.

I remain, Sir, with deep regard,

Your obedient servant,

CARLE NORMANN, R.D.N.

Copenhagen, November 18, 1865.

Extract from a Letter of CAPT. SHERARD OSBORN, R.N., C.B.

" In a nautical and physical point of view, I know of no reasons why a cable should not connect the Canadas or Labrador with England. I am fully aware that ice streams down the coast of Greenland and Iceland ; but I do not see in what way that will affect a small cable lying upon the bottom of the sea. Icefields do not prevent the Baltic being crossed with electric cables. Ice does not cut off communication across American lakes or Russian rivers ; nor did it prevent a cable being carried round the head of the Black Sea, where in the winter there is no lack of ice. Indeed, why should it ? Floe or field ice is the frozen surface of the sea ; so long as it is attached to the shore it is far less dangerous than surf or breakers would be. When it moves about it is afloat, and when afloat there is always water enough beneath it to allow a cable of half-an-inch or more in diameter to be undisturbed on the bottom of the sea.

" A floating iceberg can never hurt a submerged cable, and even one grating or pressing along the bottom may, nine cases out of ten, fail to pick up a piece of rope imbedded in the mud or sand ; indeed the probabilities are the cable would be only thrust still deeper into the bottom. Icebergs have not got claws or creepers, and I believe the cables across the narrow seas between England and Europe run fifty times more risk from the thousands of anchors, creepers, and trawling nets ever passing over them than any cable would do under the Atlantic between Hamilton Inlet and Greenland. Arctic storms are terrible ; the clash and destruction of icebergs may be awful in a winter's day off the shores of Labrador; but I do not see that they will harm a cable lying at the bottom of the sea, any more than an aurora borealis, or any other Arctic bogie would do.

"People who only consider subjects to discover difficulties, object that it may be impossible in the winter-time to lift or repair a cable between Iceland and Greenland, or Greenland and Labrador. This objection, I maintain, holds good in all transatlantic cables; for I have not yet heard of the seaman or engineer who will undertake to lift the 2,000 miles of cable between Iceland and Newfoundland at any season, much less during the winter time."

Extract from Proceedings of Royal Geographical Society.

Sir Chas. Bright, F.R.G.S., Jan. 28, 1861.

"I have only to observe, that the result of the recent survey has been to remove from my mind the apprehensions which I previously entertained in common with many others, as to the extent and character of the difficulties to be overcome in carrying a line of telegraph to America by the northern route.

"Prior to the dispatch of the surveying expedition, we had no knowledge of the depth of the seas to be crossed, with the exception of the few soundings obtained by Colonel Shaffner in 1859, and our information as to the nature of the shores of Greenland in regard to the requirements for a telegraphic cable was equally small.

"These points are of vital consequence to the prospects of the North Atlantic route, and the survey has placed us in possession of satisfactory particulars respecting them. The soundings taken by Sir Leopold M'Clintock will be a guide in the selection of the most suitable form for the deep-sea lengths of the cables, while the information furnished for Capt. Young will direct the construction of the more massive cables to be laid in the inlets of the coast. It is not necessary to determine upon the precise landing places and other points of detail in connection with the enterprise at the present time, but the promoters of the undertaking have received ample encouragement from the survey, and from the testimony of competent and experienced voyagers and sojourners in the countries to which the line is to be carried, to warrant them in proceeding with their labours with renewed vigour and confidence.

Extracted from Evidence taken before the Submarine Telegraph Committee.

Captain Sir EDWARD BELCHER, C.B., examined.

4257. (*Chairman.*) You have had considerable experience, I believe, in polar navigation, both north and south ?—On both sides of America, in Behring's Straits as well as the other side. More particularly in Behring's Straits and the banks of Newfoundland, among the icebergs.

4258. Have you formed any opinion as to the practicability of laying a cable to America by way of the Faro Islands, Iceland, Greenland, and Labrador ?—I have.

4259. Assuming that we start from England, you would go to the Faro Islands, I presume ?—I should prefer going to the Shetlands first.

4260. From the north coast of Scotland ?—From the north coast of Scotland, *via* the Orkney Islands.

4261. And from the Shetlands to the Faro Islands ?—Yes.

4262. Have you considered or observed the tides and whirlpools which are said to exist near the Faro Islands ?—I have not; nor have I witnessed any of those whirlpools on the direct passage to Greenland. I think they belong peculiarly to the islands and to the tides which belong to the islands. I consider that the tides in the vicinity of the land always differ materially from the tides off shore.

4263. Do you anticipate that there would be any liability to injury to a cable from friction on the rocks in consequence of those sides ?—I do not. I consider the information that we have at present of those islands is very imperfect, and that it is almost absurd in any person, until he does obtain the information that is requisite, as to where the banks lie, and whether those banks are mud, or sand, or rock, to assert that the thing cannot be done. I have had a great deal of experience all over the world in dealing with rocks near the land, but I never knew of any rock bottom in 100 fathoms off shore, except in the Coral Islands in the Pacific. There, I think, at 960 fathoms we lost the rock, and the bottom was found to be sand. After it has been *determined* how the rocks lie, and if there are available gullies between them, containing mud or sand, then it will be easy to place in such situations cables adapted to the cases. In all such cases (as it has been imagined apply to islands like Shetland and the Faro Islands), I would venture to suggest that you have been dealing with others much more liable to objection in the Mediterranean, and specially as to terrestial heat! I view the islands above water as merely apices of what would be disclosed if the sea receded; and if abrupt ravines discover themselves at the coast line, they may naturally be looked for as continuous below water. But being filled with mud and debris, they offer a good bed for a cable, judiciously laid, in any of these determined hollows. Therefore, I must be understood in my replies to mean, that I would not run the cable *direct* and *across ridges*, but carry it to *the communicating branch*, which I suppose would run in the meridian north and south from the positions in question.

4264. Is the mud, as a rule, deep at 100 fathoms?—I think whenever you come to mud at that depth, it is very slimy mud. In all cases where I have seen rope or any material that has been sent down in very deep water, the mud has adhered to it when it came to the surface with great tenacity, and it was very difficult to wash it off. A very peculiar sticky mud is found at great depths. I think if you were to determine the outline of the soundings at 100 fathoms, and bring the cable up into the meridian of any of those points to which you propose to carry the line, you could run it up on that meridian perfectly free from any chance of troubles from icebergs. The ice in all those regions, from Europe until you go round Cape Farewell, and get on the west side of Greenland, is merely floe ice. Floe ice, in ordinary times, should never exceed 7 feet in thickness. The law is half-an-inch, or 0·44 increase, for every day during the winter months. So that you may arrive pretty nearly to what the floe ice should be. When you find what are termed heavy floes of 21, 22, 23, or 24 feet, that results from the breaking up of the floe, and one portion pressing above another, until seven or eight layers become attached to each other, and the first thaw cements them into one mass.

4265. The floe ice I believe rises very little above the surface of the sea?—One-twelfth. I find that the immersion is ⅟ᵢths. I am taking the specific gravity that has been given us by different authorities, that would exactly make it, as nearly as possible. I see in the former voyages by Phipps that the floe ice got as high as ²¹⁄₂₂nds of immersion, some of the densest ice that they fell in with, the water being previously purged of air.

4266. Have you visited the coast of Iceland?—I have not.

4267. Along the east coast of Greenland you think there is no danger from anything but floe ice?—I think not from the account of Lieutenant Graah, the Danish navigator, he having passed along the eastern coast close inshore in an oomiak where he found the bergs calving off to sea. The water is so deep that there is no chance of bergs troubling the ground, and consequently any cable if it were carried up in a ravine in the fiords on that side would be quite safe, because the berg would strike the ground on either side of the deep gulley without troubling the cable in deep water.

4268. The bergs come from some point further to the north, do they not?—The bergs come from both sides of Greenland; they break off from the shore.

4270. Have you formed any opinion as to what point of the east coast of Greenland you would carry the cable to?—I should propose carrying it as far south as I could into the first fiord that opens.

4276. From Greenland would you go to Julianshaab?—To one of those southern fiords.

4277. And then across to Labrador?—Yes. There is a point that seems to have been overlooked hitherto, it is reported that a bank runs between Labrador and the coast of Greenland; there is a ridge somewhere which is well known to whalers to exist; a spur from Labrador which reaches across towards Greenland and turns the ice from the Labrador coast off towards Cape Farewell. The currents out of Hudson's Strait, Davis's Strait, and Cumberland Sound must tend to drive the ice out to the eastward; it meets with the eddy of the gulf-stream which deflects it to America and the Banks of Newfoundland about St. John's, but the space about the mouth of the Straits of Belleisle and around there is generally free from ice all he year round. I have been since informed that this bank extends north and south off the coast of Labrador, and the cross bank has never been satisfactorily proved. If this be the case, the tail of this meridional reef, where it affords 200 fathoms mud, would prove the best point from which to start the connection to Greenland, assuming the spaces within to be protected by the bergs which are said to ground there. I think, after mature consideration, that all the lines should be run *independently from* the *western to* the eastern stations.

4278. Along the coast of Labrador?—I do not know how far up, but I should think it would be almost up to the mouth of Hudson's Straits. I do not think there would be any ice from that region which would press on the coast of Labrador, in proof of which none of the whale ships that have been beset or destroyed by the ice have been deposited upon that shore ; therefore I suspect that the whole of that coast is kept free by the many inlets and currents on the shore.   The currents set up upon the western side of Davis Strait and down southerly upon the other and you are obliged to work up on the east side till you reach Cape York, and then cross over and come down the west side; consequently the current which is running down the western side tends to sweep out south-easterly across towards Cape Farewell.   The water about the north-east angle of Labrador is so very deep that there is no chance of any iceberg grounding there.

4279. And the ridge of which you have spoken would prevent icebergs coming out ?—It would tend to intercept the current and divert it easterly.

4280. It would intercept any icebergs which were sunk below in a great depth of water ?—If they arrive at this ridge which is supposed to run across, undoubtedly they would ground upon it and be driven off in the direction of the current.

4281. If the cable were laid south of this ridge, in your opinion, it would be protected from icebergs ?—Yes ; my idea of laying a cable is to seek a depth at which no icebergs would touch it, and just to keep on the deeper verge of that depth, working along it until you come to Newfoundland itself.   It should be attached to some vessel moored off until you have secured your communication, and then run across to Greenland.   The heavy ice never presses upon Cape Farewell, and never has been known to touch the southern part of that land at all.   My view in taking this route is not distinctly connecting it with any particular position in Labrador, but with Newfoundland at the Strait of Belle Isle, *if found convenient.*

4282. The ice is always carried round it ?—Yes.

4283. And does not touch the east side of it ?—No, I believe not.   With regard to Newfoundland, I have counted in the month of May as many as 80 icebergs at a time on the banks of Newfoundland ; and during the period I was employed there, the only berg I saw grounded off the shores of Newfoundland was in 16 fathoms. The ice is so very nicely poised, that if it was passing along the bottom I do not think that there is much chance of its raking the bottom ; it would quietly roll over as a roller would do, and impress the cable into the ground instead of damaging it ; it would not rut the ground up.   The moment it touches the bottom you can observe it turn over directly as easily as possible, from the very nature of its construction. The temperature of the sea beneath is always about 36 degrees to 38 degrees, consequently it must be thawing; and as the under part of the ice is always in a thawing state, there would be no edges to cut.

4285. Your opinion is, that it would be very feasible to lay and maintain a cable along the coast between England and America, by the route of Iceland, Labrador, and Greenland?—Yes; I can tell you a little more about the bottom of the sea on the west side of Greenland, because I dredged along this coast, working up to Disco from the southward, and I found it all mud even in about 15 or 16 fathoms. There is a bank off Holsteinberg, which is composed of fine sand, where they catch great quantities of cod.

4287. Off the south point of Iceland, is not there a certain amount of volcanic bank, on which, as late as 1830, a volcano was seen, or smoke was seen, issuing from the sea?—I do not know, but we had Graham's Island thrown up off the coast of Sicily, but it has gone down, and there is a *sand bank* instead of it. I think the same objection, if it be made, applies equally to all portions of the ocean depths, and more particularly to the Mediterranean. But how it is to be discovered, beyond absolute test perpendicularly above the spot, I am at a loss to comprehend.

4288. Would not that be rather an unsafe place to lay a cable, in case the island might come up again?—I do not know that; it would depend upon the temperature of the water around. If the temperature of the water around there is high, why the further off (in deep water) the cable is the better.

4289. From the south coast of Iceland to near Cape Farewell? —I would run it as nearly as possible in the parallel until it arrives near the land. I would then take it into some of the fiords across there. From Graah's account, there is no ice here during the early summer months. There is the floe ice, which is attached to the land, but it cannot be of any importance, because whenever a heavy breeze sets in, the effect of the sea working under the floe detaches it and breaks it up. From none of those fiords being clearly laid down, there can be no route determined through the floe. About August it is free from ice.

4290. Still, the northern part of the east coast of Greenland is entirely locked up with ice, is not it?—It has not been satisfactorily examined. Here is Graah's Island, where he stopped; but then he had nothing but a skin boat, a thing that in the seaway twists and turns in every manner. You can hardly make use of it at all. I know that the oomiak is a very difficult thing to handle in a seaway. In some of the northern portions of Greenland Scoresby says that he saw grass land. In the month of June he had grass and very hot weather. On the other side of America, at Behring's Straits, you have ice, and at Blossom shoals I observed ice aground in 20 fathoms; but that is the deepest water in which I ever saw ice aground on that side; that is in 120 feet water. I do not think that the experience of Graah in an open oomiak, a mere skin boat, can be assumed as a guide as to the ice to be dealt with on the east coast of Greenland. I am, however, inclined to think that it will be imperative to watch carefully for the period to start from Greenland, and connect with the vessel lying off. Also that the question of connecting it again with Iceland should be secured by some beacon off shore, if it should happen that heavy westerly gales prevented running into port. These are matters demanding the most scrupulous investigation, and of infinite interest to navigation should our ships be stationed in that neighbourhood.

4297. (*Chairman.*) Are there no currents between Labrador and Greenland which would be injurious to laying a cable?—There are no ocean currents, I think, that would trouble any cable in any part of that region that I know of.

4312. You think there is very little to be feared from ice between England and Greenland?—During the whole passage from the Orkneys to Cape Farewell I did not meet with a single berg until we got within 300 miles of Cape Farewell, and that was only a little bit of ice, it was no berg.

4313. Between Greenland and Labrador the bank which you mentioned would protect the cable from bergs?—The bank that runs round Cape Farewell and runs up that coast would protect the cable completely, because the evidence given by the Danes on that coast is, that no icebergs ever ground on the west coast of Greenland. It is off shore that they can see it pass, but then it is probably in 1,500 or 2,000 fathoms.

4314. What was the greatest depth of sounding that you took between Labrador and Greenland?—I never obtained any deeper sounding than 60 fathoms.

4315. That was further to the north I suppose?—It was along the coast southerly and abreast of Holsteinberg.

4316. Have you been by Hamilton's Inlet at all?—No; I do not know anything of it. The greatest measured height of any

iceberg that I ever saw was 150 feet as a pinnacle, and when it
canted, or turned bottom upwards, it was not above 80 feet.

4320. Assuming a line of cable to be laid down, do you imagine
that it could be all laid in several sections at the same time of the
year, or would you select a different period of the year for laying
each section?—I think it could be all laid at the same period of
the year, but I think each portion should be laid separately.

4321. I mean whether the season of the year which was favourable for laying one section would be favourable for laying another
section; for example, whether on the east coast of Greenland, the
same period of the year would be as favourable a one as it would
be for laying it on the west coast of Greenland?—That is the only
point that I feel any doubt about, namely, the period at which you
can get it to or from the east coast of Greenland—that we are none
of us aware of; neither Graah nor any other person who has been
there has solved that question.   Therefore, until that is determined
I should not be disposed to give an opinion, but my conviction is,
that between August and October anything that can be done should
be done in those months, but you may work upon all other points
from May until October.   The ordinary period of receiving our in-
structions for northern work from the Admiralty is to quit London
in March.

4322. Do you imagine that if stations were established in
Greenland and Labrador the present colonists would be available
for the purpose of keeping up those stations during the winter, or
that we should have to send out colonists?—I should think on the
Labrador coast you would have about as highly-civilized a set of
natives as you will find in almost any other part of the world.

4323. And in Greenland?—In Greenland they are very fair.

4324. Of course they are Danish?—Yes, a mixed race.   They
have schools, and they are very well clothed, and are perfectly
under command; there is not the slightest attempt at opposition.
They are thoroughly under the Danish government, and if the
Danish government gave an order, no matter what it was, however
impossible apparently to us English, they would have it done; they
are very strict with them.

THE NORTH ATLANTIC TELEGRAPH.

The desirability of establishing telegraphic communication between America and Europe is universally recognised. There are great public works against the execution of which political objections may be urged; but the establishment of telegraphic communication with America is not only unobjectionable to any nation in the world —it is favoured and commended by every Government in Europe and America. England and Russia, France and America, Germany and Denmark are here at one.

On this subject there is neither rivalry nor jealousy. We may have our preferences for this route or that route; but every route that promises to complete the connection between the Old World and the New is impartially favoured by the public of both continents. How popular the enterprise really is, was proved last summer by the interest with which we all watched the expedition of the Great Eastern.

The successive failures of the schemes to lay a cable from Ireland to Newfoundland, while they have not diminished the public interest in the chivalrous labours of the company which has charge of that enterprise, have nevertheless led practical men to turn their attention to other means of accomplishing the object desired.

Telegraphists, fortunately, are not restricted to a single route. Four routes are available—the route to the west, direct from Ireland to Newfoundland; that to the east, through the vast deserts of the Russian Empire; that to the south, by way of Gibraltar, the coast of Africa, and the Cape Verde Islands; and that to the north, from Scotland to Iceland, from Iceland to Greenland, and from Greenland to Labrador. The last route, it has long seemed to us, presents the fewest difficulties. Without disparaging in the least the work of the Russian Company, without even seeming to despise the new efforts about to be made by the Anglo-American Company, we cannot help expressing our satisfaction that a company has been formed to utilize the advantages of the northern route.

The North Atlantic project possesses over the other projects we have mentioned certain undoubted advantages. The route is shorter than the Russian, less hazardous than the direct route. Instead of one cable thousands of miles long, the North Atlantic scheme requires four cables, varying in length from 750 to 240 miles each. More speedily laid, more easily repaired, the cables of the northern route would also be more effective as a means of communication than the cable of the Anglo-American line. The total length of the submerged wires in the one case would not be much greater than in that of the other. From Scotland to the Faroe Islands, the distance is 250 miles; from the Faroes to Iceland, 240; from Iceland to Greenland, 743; and from Greenland to Labrador, 507. As the submersion of each length of cable would occupy only a few days, the risk attending the operation would be comparatively small. Even in the event of accident, the loss would in no case exceed 743 miles. The whole route has been more than once surveyed, and the depth of sea and the character of the sea-bottoms have been sufficiently well-ascertained. The commanders and surveyors of different expeditions have all reported on the practicability of the whole route. Indeed, the authorities on the nature of the Arctic seas—men of experience and skill--are remarkably unanimous on the subject.

But objections have been urged that icebergs would damage the cable, and that the excessive cold of Iceland and Greenland would interfere with the electric current. The testimony of well-known navigators, however, is a sufficient answer to these objections. It is only in shallow waters near the coasts that icebergs would at all affect the cables, and the difficulty in such cases, we have the authority of Captain ALLEN YOUNG, Sir LEOPOLD M'CLINTOCK, and of Captain SHERARD OSBORN for saying, could easily be obviated. As to the climatic objection, it has been proved that telegraphic lines work even better in cold climates than in warm latitudes. When KELLETT and M'CLINTOCK were beset in the ice far to the north of the Arctic zone, they communicated with each other by telegraph from ship to ship. That telegraph was at work the whole winter, and was in no way affected by the intense cold experienced in those rigorous latitudes.

It follows, therefore, that the chief objections raised to the North

Atlantic route have really no existence in fact. The expense of working the northern line would of course be greater than that of working the Atlantic line, because telegraph stations would have to be established at the termination of each section of the cable. The duty of the clerks at these stations, however, would be merely nominal, while the increased power of the electric current obtained would enable far more words to be transmitted in a given time by the one route than by the other. It would not be necessary, we are informed, to retransmit the through messages at each point of junction, because repeating instruments, with relays of auxiliary battery power, would be placed at the different land stations. England could therefore communicate with America without a break of line, just as now messages can be transmitted from London to Constantinople or Vienna. All that the clerks at each station in ordinary times would have to do would be to secure the safe transmission of the messages.

The commercial value of the enterprise depends of course on the speed with which messages can be sent from one end of the line to the other. In this respect the northern route possesses undoubted advantages over the direct route. It appears to be an established law that the speed of transmission of all submarine cables is in proportion to their length. "Should the North Atlantic cable be successfully laid," says Professor WHEATSTONE, "there can be no doubt of the great advantage it would have in one important respect—that by means of its separate portions a more speedy communication of intelligence would be effected than by the long sea route." Messages at the rate of two words and a half per minute were transmitted through the Atlantic cable which was successfully submerged in 1858; but it is calculated that fifteen words per minute could be sent by the North Atlantic line. The more rapid communication by means of the latter route would enable the company not only to establish a lower tariff, but to realise a larger revenue. While in the one case, at 5s. per word, an annual revenue of £180,000 could be realised, in the other, at 2s. 6d. per word, a revenue of no less than £540,000 per annum could be secured.

With these facts, testimonies, and calculations before us, it is scarcely to doubt that the northern enterprise is not only perfectly practicable, but reasonably certain of commercial success.

The scheme of establishing a telegraphic communication with America by way of Iceland and Greenland is not at all a new project. It has been more or less before the public for the last fourteen years. In 1852, Mr. JAMES WYLD, M.P., obtained the sanction of the Danish Government to carry a line through the Danish territories. No use was made of this sanction, and in 1854 Colonel SHAFFNER, of Kentucky, secured a concession from the same Government for the same purpose. SHAFFNER himself in 1859 surveyed the whole route at his own expense; but for some reason or other he failed to utilise the concession he had obtained. In the meantime M'CLINTOCK and ALLEN YOUNG were despatched on surveying expeditions by the English Government. Last year, Colonel SHAFFNER having relinquished his concessions, the Danish Government granted permission to Mr. WYLD and certain gentlemen associated with him, to lay down telegraphic cables throughout the Danish provinces in Europe and America.

It is to make use of the handsome concession of the Danish authorities, that a new telegraphic company has now been formed. To this Company, known as the North Atlantic Telegraph Company, Mr. N. J. HOLMES is engineer. Need we say that we wish the new enterprise all possible success?

Different details of the revised scheme of WYLD and SHAFFNER have been approved by men of acknowledged eminence in science and adventure. Sir RODERICK MURCHISON, General SABINE, Professor WHEATSTONE, Sir EDWARD BELCHER, Captain SHERARD OSBORN, Sir LEOPOLD M'CLINTOCK, Captain ALLEN YOUNG, Dr. REA, and Admiral FITZROY, have all expressed their approbation of the project.

Endorsed by authorities such as these, the North Atlantic scheme is almost independent of even public approval. The project of opening telegraphic communication with America no longer depends upon the successful submerging of a cable, thousands of miles long. Two admirable schemes for compassing the same desirable object are now before the world. Both deserve success, and both, let us impartially hope, will ultimately attain it.—*Newcastle Daily Chronicle March 23rd*, 1866.